WITHDRAWN

10/05

First Facts™

From Farm to Table

From Cane to Sugar

by Roberta Basel

Consultant:
Art Hill, Professor of Food Science
University of Guelph
Guelph, Ontario, Canada

Capstone
press

Mankato, Minnesota

First Facts is published by Capstone Press,
151 Good Counsel Drive, P.O. Box 669, Mankato, Minnesota 56002.
www.capstonepress.com

Library of Congress Cataloging-in-Publication Data
Basel, Roberta.
   From cane to sugar / by Roberta Basel.
   p. cm.—(First facts. From farm to table)
   Includes bibliographical references (p. 23) and index.
   Summary: "An introduction to the basic concept of food production, distribution,
and consumption by tracing the production of sugar from sugarcane to the finished
product"—Provided by publisher.
   ISBN 0-7368-4283-7 (hardcover)
   1. Sugar—Juvenile literature. 2. Sugarcane—Juvenile literature. I. Title. II. Series.
TP378.2.B37 2006
664'.122—dc22
                                                            2004029135

Editorial Credits

Jennifer Besel, editor; Jennifer Bergstrom, set designer; Ted Williams, book designer;
   Wanda Winch, photo researcher/photo editor

Photo Credits

Capstone Press/Karon Dubke, cover, 1, 5, 19, 21
Comstock, back cover
Corbis/Eye Ubiquitous/Bruce Adams, 10; Philip Gould, 12–13, 15; Tony Arruza, 14, 16–17
Grant Heilman Photography, 8–9
John Elk III, 6–7
Photo courtesy of the U.S. Sugar Corporation, 11
Richard Hamilton Smith, 20

1 2 3 4 5 6 10 09 08 07 06 05

Table of Contents

Sweet Eats

Most people eat sugar every day. It can be cooked in food such as sugar cookies. Some people put it on fruit or cereal. Sugar makes food taste sweet.

Sugar has to be made before people can eat it. Making sugar takes many steps.

Fun Fact!
All fruits and vegetables have a natural kind of sugar. Plants make sugar to store energy.

Sugarcane

Most sugar is made from sugarcane. Sugarcane is a tall type of grass. The cane can grow up to 20 feet (6 meters) tall.

Sugarcane needs warm, rainy weather. The weather in countries like Brazil and India is good for growing sugarcane.

 Fun Fact!
People in India have been making sugar out of sugarcane for more than 2,500 years.

Growing Cane

Farmers plant small pieces of old sugarcane. New sugarcane grows from these pieces.

When the cane is ready, **machines** or people cut it down. They take off the tops and leaves. Trucks, carts, or trains carry the sugarcane to the **mill**.

 Fun Fact!
Sugarcane is grown in four U.S. states. These states are Florida, Hawaii, Louisiana, and Texas.

At the Mill

Sugarcane is washed and cut at the mill. Rollers crush the cane and squeeze out the juice. The juice is then cleaned to take out dirt.

After being cleaned, the juice is
cooked in large pans. It becomes a
thick, brown syrup. Sugar **crystals**
form in the syrup.

Raw Sugar

The crystals and syrup are poured into spinning baskets. The spinning pulls crystals away from the syrup. The crystals are then dried.

Dried crystals are called raw sugar. **Factories** buy the raw sugar to make it into white sugar.

! Fun Fact!
Sugar is made in 121 countries.

13

Making White Sugar

At the factory, raw sugar is put in water. The water washes the sugar. As it's washed, raw sugar turns into a clear liquid. Then the liquid is cooked.

As the liquid cooks, many sizes of sugar crystals form. The liquid and crystals are again pulled apart in spinning baskets. The sugar is then dried. Now, the sugar is clean and white.

To the Store

Machines and people sort the different sizes of crystals. The sugar is then poured into bags.

The factories sell bags of sugar to stores. Airplanes, trains, and trucks carry sugar to the stores.

Fun Fact!
Small amounts of sugar are used to make leather, plastic, and some kinds of ink.

Where to Find Sugar

Sugar is sold almost everywhere food is sold. Grocery stores sell many different kinds of sugar. Sugar can be in the form of crystals, powder, or even cubes.

Fun Fact!
People in Brazil eat more sugar than people in any other country.

Amazing but True!

Not all sugar comes from sugarcane. About 40 percent of the world's sugar comes from sugar beets. Sugar beets are grown in fields by farmers. The root of the beet contains sugar. After processing, sugar from a sugar beet is exactly the same as sugar from sugarcane.

Hands On: Sweet American Flag

You can use sugar to make art. Follow the directions to make an American flag out of sugar cubes.

What You Need

glue
white paper, 8½ inches x 11 inches
    (22 cm x 28 cm)
cardboard, 8½ inches x 11 inches
    (22 cm x 28 cm)
small paint brush
234 sugar cubes
blue and red food coloring
50 small star stickers

What You Do

1. Glue the white paper onto the piece of cardboard.
2. With the paint brush, paint the tops of 56 sugar cubes with a small amount of blue food coloring.
3. Paint the tops of 94 sugar cubes with a small amount of red food coloring. Let the cubes sit separately overnight so the colors don't bleed.
4. Start by gluing the blue cubes to the upper left corner of the paper. Make a rectangle 8 cubes across by 7 cubes down.
5. Glue 10 red cubes across the top of the paper. Continue gluing white and red stripes down the paper to make 13 stripes.
6. Put the star stickers on the blue sugar cubes.

Glossary

crystal (KRISS-tuhl)—an object that forms a pattern of flat surfaces when it become a solid

factory (FAK-tuh-ree)—a building where products are made in large numbers; factories often use machines to make products.

machine (muh-SHEEN)—a piece of equipment that is used to do a job

mill (MIL)—a building that has machines that crush sugarcane to make raw sugar

Read More

Braithwaite, Jill. *From Cane to Sugar*. Start to Finish. Minneapolis: Lerner Publications, 2004.

Franck, Irene M., and David Brownstone. *Sugar*. Riches of the Earth. Danbury, Conn.: Grolier, 2003.

Internet Sites

FactHound offers a safe, fun way to find Internet sites related to this book. All of the sites on FactHound have been researched by our staff.

Here's how:
1. Visit *www.facthound.com*
2. Type in this special code **0736842837** for age-appropriate sites. Or enter a search word related to this book for a more general search.
3. Click on the **Fetch It** button.

FactHound will fetch the best sites for you!

Index